D1537876

J
943
Adl

Adler, Anne
Getting to know Germany

$7.95

DATE DUE			

GERMANY

Anne Adler

PASSPORT BOOKS
a division of *NTC Publishing Group*
Lincolnwood, Illinois USA

Editor: Karin Fancett (Format Publishing Services)
Design: Tony Truscott
        Edward Kinsey
Illustrations: Hayward Art Group
Consultant: Keith Lye

Photographs: Chris Fairclough, ZEFA, Leslie
Bishop, Braun, Camera Press, C.O.I. Photos, Zoë
Dominic, German Federal Railways, German
National Tourist Office, Foto Jachsse, Keystone
Press Agency, Lufthansa-Bildarchiv, The
Mansell Collection, National Gallery, Popperfoto,
C. Stadtler, ZDF

Front cover: Chris Fairclough, ZEFA
Back cover: ZEFA

This edition first published in 1990 by Passport Books,
a division of NTC Publishing Group,
4255 West Touhy Avenue, Lincolnwood (Chicago), Illinois 60646-1975 U.S.A.
Copyright © 1990, 1986 Franklin Watts Limited.
Library of Congress Catalog Card Number: 89-61900

Contents

DENMARK

North Sea

Frisian Islands

Flensburg

Kiel

Lübeck

Hamburg

Baltic Sea

POLAND

R. Weser

Lüneburg Heath

Bremen

THE NETHERLANDS

Hanover

Brunswick

Münster

Bielefeld

WEST GERMANY
(FEDERAL REPUBLIC OF GERMANY)

Harz Mountains

R. Elbe

N

West
Berlin

East
Berlin

EAST GERMANY
(GERMAN DEMOCRATIC REPUBLIC)

Duisburg

Dortmund

Essen

R. Ruhr

Düsseldorf

Cologne

Aachen

Bonn

BELGIUM

R. Rhine

R. Moselle

Taunus Mountains

Frankfurt

Wiesbaden

R. Main

LUXEMBOURG

CZECHOSLOVAKIA

Mannheim

Nuremburg

Bohemian Forest

R. Neckar

Karlsruhe

R. Danube

FRANCE

Stuttgart

R. Isar

Black Forest

Augsburg

R. Inn

0   20   40   60   80 miles

0   40   80   120 km

Scale: 1:2,500,000

Munich

Salzburg

Freiburg

SWITZERLAND

Alps

AUSTRIA

Introduction

West Germany lies in the heart of Europe. It shares borders with nine other countries and has close ties with many of its neighbors. These include strong trade links, especially with the Netherlands and France, and language links with Austria and Switzerland as well as East Germany.

For much of its history Germany consisted of numerous small states, but in 1871 it became one country, only to be divided again after World War II. The present division into East and West Germany reflects, in many ways, the uneasy relationship between the eastern and western superpowers.

Over the centuries, Germans have made many valuable contributions to European culture and there have been many great German philosophers, musicians and writers. Germans have always felt proud of their country and its traditions, but this pride was much shaken by events earlier this century – Hitler's fascist dictatorship and World War II. After the war much rebuilding was needed, but now West Germany has established itself as a strong and respected modern industrial nation.

Above: Traditional figures, like the towncrier of Lübeck, can still be seen in many parts of West Germany.

Below: Like most German cities Bonn has many new buildings. Extensive rebuilding was necessary after World War II.

The land

The West German landscape is very varied in character, ranging from Alpine mountains to the low coastal plain. The three main geographical regions are the Alpine Foothills in the south, the German Plain or Lowland in the north, and the Central Uplands in the middle of the country.

Germany's share of the Alps is very small, yet there are peaks nearly 3,000 m (10,000 ft) high. The peaks and deep valleys with wild mountain streams produce a dramatic landscape. The Alpine Foothills, further north, are much more gentle in character. The average height of this region is about 500 m (1,650 ft) and there are many rivers, lakes and moors. It is the most popular tourist area in Germany.

The Central Uplands is by far the largest landscape region in the country. The area consists of high plains, hills and valleys, and there are also many large forests in this region.

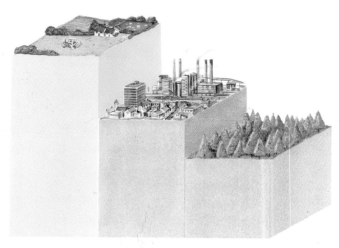

Agriculture 48% **Others** 31% **Forestry** 21%

Above: Despite Germany's industrial image, about half of its total land area is farmed. There are also large areas of forest in West Germany.

Below: The ornate castle of Hohenschwangau overlooks the Alpsee and Schwansee, two of the many lakes in the Alpine Foothills.

Above: The steep-sided valley of the Rhine near Bacharach in central Germany.

Below: These arable fields are typical of the scenery in the Central Uplands region.

The Central Uplands also has mountainous areas, such as the Swabian–Franconian Alps and the Black Forest (in the south and southwest) and the Harz Mountains (near the frontier with East Germany). Some of the mountains rise to 1,000 m (3,300 ft) and more.

To the west of the Black Forest the wide valley of the Rhine extends from the Swiss border to the Taunus Mountains near Frankfurt am Main. North of Frankfurt the Rhine valley is much narrower, winding through a mountainous area of the Central Uplands until Cologne, where the valley widens again. The Rhine is the most important north–south axis in West Germany and also the longest river in the country.

The Lowland is a vast plain, bordering on the North and Baltic Seas. Apart from a few hills in the Lüneburg heathland, the land is very flat. Scattered along Germany's North Sea coast there are many small islands which are together known as the Frisian Islands. The Baltic coastline is flat and sandy in parts, but has steep cliffs elsewhere.

The people

If you ask people from Munich to describe themselves, the chances are that they will say they are Bavarians rather than Germans. Until 1871 the area known as West Germany was a collection of separate independent states, and even today many of these regions still keep a sense of separate identity.

An example of these regional differences is that everyday speech heard on the street varies considerably from one area to another. Bavarians visiting the city of Cologne, for example, may have difficulty making themselves understood, and will themselves have difficulty with the dialect of Cologne. They will probably resort to using High German (*Hochdeutsch*). This is the standard language, as used in the media and in schools.

Most Germans are descended from the ancient tribes of the region, such as the Saxons and Frisians of the north, and the Bavarians and Swabians of the south. Although there has been much mixing of the groups over the centuries some original characteristics may have survived.

Above: Older Germans, like this couple, are likely to have experienced many dramatic changes in Germany during their lifetime.

Below: Germans born since World War II are more informal, both in their style of dress and their outlook on life, than previous generations.

Above: Hans Zimmermann sells sausages.

Below: Wolf-Dieter Löbe is a police officer.

Above: Waltraud Ettinger works in a florist's shop.

Below: Hermann Schäfer delivers the mail.

Northerners, it is said, are blue-eyed, sober and hardworking. Their towns are full of stern, brick buildings. By contrast, the southerners are of a darker complexion, and are thought to be more easy-going and more talkative. Their buildings are often ornate and colorful. Regional differences are also reflected in religion: the north is mainly Protestant, while the south is mostly Roman Catholic.

After World War II many families moved from East to West Germany. During the period between 1955 and 1961 alone there were over two million migrants from East to West Germany compared with only around 280,000 in the other direction. During the 1950s and 1960s there were also large influxes of foreign workers (or *Gastarbeiter*) from countries such as Italy, Greece and Turkey.

The Germans have the reputation of being a formal people, fond of rules and regulations. To some extent this is still true, but far less so among the younger generation who have grown up in the last 20 or 30 years.

Above: Gisela Thode manages a wine bar.

Below: Günter Hanisch, a foreign-language teacher.

Where people live

West Germany is one of the most crowded countries in the world. On average, there are 245 inhabitants to every square kilometer (0.4 square miles) of land. The most densely populated part of the country is the highly industrialized Ruhr area. Nine per cent of the population live here in cities such as Essen and Dortmund. Other crowded regions include the suburbs of the major cities: Munich, Frankfurt am Main, Cologne and Hamburg.

As in other parts of Europe, the number of people working on the land is in decline because agriculture has become more efficient. More and more people are moving from rural to urban areas in search of work. Although there are only three cities in West Germany with populations of over a million (Hamburg, West Berlin and Munich), over half the population lives in towns of over 20,000 inhabitants.

When the country of West Germany was founded in 1949, the small town of Bonn was declared the capital. Bonn has remained one of the smaller cities of West Germany.

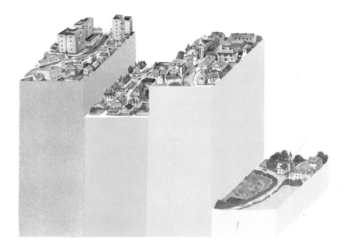

Cities
35%

Large towns
26%

Small towns
33%

Villages
6%

Above: Over a third of the West German population live in the 70 or so cities which have over 100,000 people.

Below: Ranschbach is an old settlement in one of the wine-growing regions. All the houses cluster around the village church.

Left: Dortmund, a city in the Ruhr area.
Below: Munich is West Germany's third largest city.

Above: Many Germans live in rented apartments, such as these in Mannheim, but most would prefer their own house.

There is no dominant city. Each major city is important for different reasons. Frankfurt is a commercial center, the headquarters of no less than 350 banks. Many publishing firms and virtually the whole of the German film industry are based in Munich. Hamburg, with its huge port, is one of Germany's great trading cities. Even small provincial towns have a lot to offer, so nobody need travel too far to enjoy good entertainment or to go shopping.

Many buildings were destroyed during World War II, and some 16 million new dwellings have been built since 1949. Many of these are high-rise blocks of flats. About half of the population live in houses, either as tenants or owners. As elsewhere in Europe, there was a movement away from the inner-city areas to the growing suburbs during the 1960s and 1970s, but now, to some extent, this trend is being reversed.

West Berlin

Berlin became the capital of a united Germany in 1871. At the end of World War II, in 1945, the Allies divided the ruined city into four sectors, each one to be administered by one of the victorious powers – Britain, France, the USA and the USSR. Four years later the arrangements were changed and the USSR became responsible for East Berlin, and the other three powers for West Berlin.

As political tensions grew between eastern and western Europe, West Berlin found itself in an extraordinary position: it was entirely surrounded by the unfriendly new state of East Germany of which the eastern sector of Berlin was now the capital. West Berlin belonged to West Germany, whose capital was at Bonn, hundreds of miles away to the west. For a time, the only way westerners could reach West Berlin was by air.

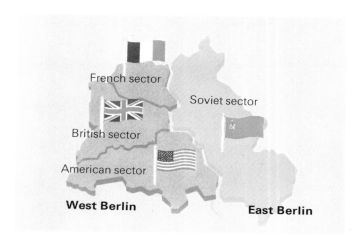

Above: Berlin is divided into four sectors, three of them in the West. Both East and West Berlin have populations of over a million people.

Below: The city of Berlin needed extensive rebuilding after World War II. Over half the city was destroyed but a few older buildings did survive.

In August 1961 the East Germans built a wall right across the middle of Berlin, cutting themselves off from the West. The wall was, and still is, heavily guarded, and many East Germans died trying to cross it.

Today the wall still stands. Foreign visitors are allowed limited access to the eastern sector through one of the checkpoints, and more recently West Germans and West Berliners, too, are allowed in on special permits to visit relatives.

West Berlin is the 11th federal state of West Germany, although this status is not recognized by the East Germans. Representatives are sent to the parliament (*Bundestag*) in Bonn, but they have limited powers.

West Berlin is a lively cultural centre, famous for opera, music, theater and cinema, and its university. Its broad shopping streets are lined with cafes and restaurants. The city also has many lakes and woodlands, where the Berliners love to spend their weekends. However, despite its often relaxed air, the city is still uncertain of its future, and many younger inhabitants leave for the greater security of other parts of West Germany.

Above left: Both Berliners and tourists like to shop in the Kurfürstendamm.

Above: Touring the city aboard the *Moby Dick.*

Below: A British soldier on patrol in West Berlin. Behind him is the famous Brandenburg Gate and part of the Berlin Wall.

Fact file: land and population

Key facts

Location: West Germany, a nation in western Europe, lies between latitudes 47°30′ and 55° North and longitudes 6° and 14° East. It is bordered by nine other countries: The Netherlands, Belgium, Luxembourg, France, Switzerland, Austria, Czechoslovakia, East Germany and Denmark. It has short coastlines on the Baltic and North Seas.

Main parts: Germany contains ten states, plus West Berlin, an area of 480 sq km (185 sq miles), which is surrounded by East Germany.

Area: 248,577 sq km (95,976 sq miles).

Population: 60,824,000 (1987 estimate). West Germany has a larger population than any other European country, except for the USSR.

Capital city: Bonn

Major cities (with English and German names in 1986 populations):

  West Berlin (1,869,000)
  Hamburg (1,576,000)
  Munich (München, 1,269,000)
  Cologne (Köln, 914,000)
  Essen (618,000)
  Frankfurt am Main (593,000)
  Dortmund (570,000)
  Stuttgart (565,000)
  Düsseldorf (561,000)
  Bremen (525,000)
  Duisburg (517,000)
  Hanover (Hannover, 506,000)
  Nuremberg (Nürnberg, 467,000)

Language: High (Standard) German. German is one of the Germanic language family, which also includes Dutch and English.

Highest point: Zugspitze, 2,968 m (9,738 ft), on the Austrian border.

Major rivers: The Danube rises in the southwest and then flows east through seven other countries before it reaches the Black Sea. The Rhine, West Germany's most important river, rises in Switzerland. Its total length is 1,320 km (820 miles). Other leading rivers are the Elbe, which is 1,167 km (725 miles) long; and the Weser, 500 km (311 miles) long.

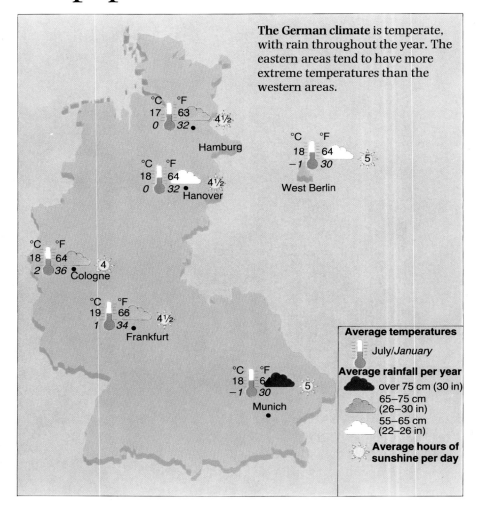

The German climate is temperate, with rain throughout the year. The eastern areas tend to have more extreme temperatures than the western areas.

°C 17 / 0   °F 63 / 32   4½ — Hamburg

°C 18 / 0   °F 64 / 32   4½ — Hanover

°C 18 / −1   °F 64 / 30   5 — West Berlin

°C 18 / 2   °F 64 / 36   4 — Cologne

°C 19 / 1   °F 66 / 34   4½ — Frankfurt

°C 18 / −1   °F 6 / 30   5 — Munich

Average temperatures
July/*January*

Average rainfall per year
over 75 cm (30 in)
65–75 cm (26–30 in)
55–65 cm (22–26 in)

Average hours of sunshine per day

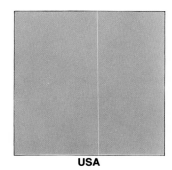

USA   Australia   W. Germany   UK

△ **A land area comparison**
West Germany's land area of 248,577 sq km (95,976 sq miles) is small in comparison with many other countries. It is only about 1/40th of the size of the USA (9,370,000 sq km, 3,600,000 sq miles) and also much smaller than Australia (7,650,000 sq km,

2,470,000 sq miles). It is very similar in size to the United Kingdom (244,030 sq km, 94,220 sq miles). The longest north–south distance in West Germany is 853 km (530 miles), the longest east–west distance is 453 km (281 miles).

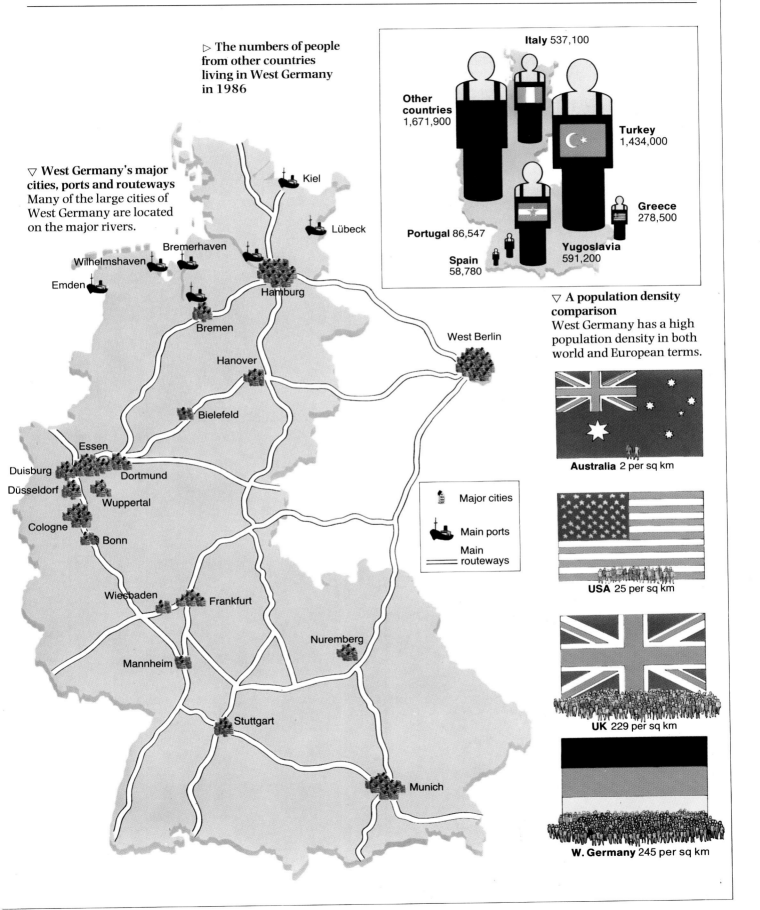

▷ **The numbers of people from other countries living in West Germany in 1986**

Italy 537,100

Other countries 1,671,900

Turkey 1,434,000

Portugal 86,547

Spain 58,780

Yugoslavia 591,200

Greece 278,500

▽ **West Germany's major cities, ports and routeways**
Many of the large cities of West Germany are located on the major rivers.

Kiel

Lübeck

Bremerhaven

Wilhelmshaven

Emden

Hamburg

Bremen

Hanover

West Berlin

Bielefeld

Essen

Duisburg

Dortmund

Düsseldorf

Wuppertal

Cologne

Bonn

Wiesbaden

Frankfurt

Mannheim

Nuremberg

Stuttgart

Munich

Major cities

Main ports

Main routeways

▽ **A population density comparison**
West Germany has a high population density in both world and European terms.

Australia 2 per sq km

USA 25 per sq km

UK 229 per sq km

W. Germany 245 per sq km

Home life

The Germans tend to be a home-loving people, and take great pride in keeping their houses neat and orderly. About 10 per cent of household income is generally spent on decorating and furnishing the home and both modern and traditional styles are popular.

Most families are small and live in compact houses and apartments,. Usually there is a kitchen, a bathroom, a living room and one or two bedrooms. Dwellings built in the last 15 years have been designed to a high standard, normally with central heating and with modern kitchens that include a refrigerator and a washing machine. Young children often share bedrooms. The traditional German bed-covering is a thick comforter known as a *Federbett*, which is soft, comfortable and very warm.

The working day starts early in Germany. Factories often start at about 7 a.m., and most shops, offices and schools are open by 8. So it is quite common for all the family to have left the house by half past seven in the morning.

Above: The Marschkes own a modern house on an estate outside Pliezhausen, a small town in southern Germany.

Below: The Marschkes's back garden, where the children play and their parents pursue their interest in gardening.

Left: As well as the living room shown here, the Marschkes's house has a dining room, four bedrooms, and a kitchen and bathroom.

Below: The two younger children, Simon and Silja, share a bedroom which also doubles as a playroom. Their elder sister Gundula has her own room, but still likes to use the playroom too.

Working hours tend to be quite long: an industrial worker, for instance, spends just over 40 hours a week at his or her job. There is, however, one consolation: Germany has many public holidays.

Most schools end between 12 noon and 1 p.m. and children go home to lunch. If the mother or father's place of work is close to home, they, too, will eat at home. After lunch the children will have homework to do, but once this is complete they can play or watch television.

Traditionally, the role of German women was confined to the three "K's": *Kirche* (church), *Küche* (kitchen) and *Kinder* (children). Today women are equal to men before the law, and account for approximately a third of the entire workforce. Even so, in many families it is still the male who is able to earn a higher salary and the woman who stays at home to do the housework and look after the children. As elsewhere in Europe, many German women are now challenging their traditional roles.

Shops and shopping

West Germany was one of the first countries to provide pedestrian malls in town centers, areas where one can stroll from shop to shop without having to worry about traffic. Shopping centers often take in a mixture of large department stores and small specialized shops. Many Germans prefer the latter, because they offer goods of higher quality and more personal attention from the staff. Even the smallest gift will be elaborately wrapped.

From Monday to Friday, shops in West Germany stay open until around 6 p.m. On Saturday most shops close at lunchtime, although on one Saturday each month they remain open until later.

Fruit and vegetables are usually bought from street markets which are held once or twice a week. Often it is the farmers themselves who set up the stalls, so everything is very fresh. Throughout December, many towns have special Christmas markets (*Weihnachtsmärkte*) with stalls selling everything from seasonal goodies to candles and Christmas trees.

Above: A selection of German packaged foods. Most families do the bulk of their shopping at the local supermarket.

Below: Nuremberg, like most other German cities, has a regular market where fruit and vegetables may be bought.

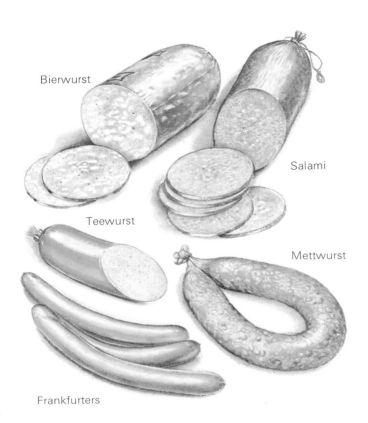

Bierwurst

Salami

Teewurst

Mettwurst

Frankfurters

Above: A butcher's shop.

Left: There are about 1,500 types of German sausage.

Below: Clothes are often cheaper in department stores than in small shops, and there is usually more choice, too.

Supermarkets and hypermarkets are as popular as elsewhere in Europe and the USA, but small local shops continue to exist and have actually become more popular again in recent years.

The butcher's shop (*Metzgerei*) sells raw meat, as well as a variety of the sausages for which Germany is famous, and other cooked meats. The bakery (*Bäckerei*) normally bakes bread on the premises and offers a great range from crusty white rolls to rye bread and wholemeal loaves. For pastries, cakes and chocolates, one goes to a shop called a *Konditorei*. These shops often have a cafe attached to them, where one can sit down for coffee and cakes or a small snack. Most *Konditoreien* are open on Sundays.

Electrical goods are a bargain in many West German shops, with quality goods at low prices backed up with efficient servicing. Germany also has a long tradition of manufacturing and selling quality toys and the children's department of a big store often resembles an Aladdin's cave.

Cooking and eating

In Germany the day starts with a cup of fresh coffee and crisp rolls or sliced bread with butter or jam. Sometimes this light breakfast might include a boiled egg. Because people often have to leave home early in the morning, it is common to have a sandwich and a drink as a mid-morning snack.

The main meal of the day is usually eaten at lunchtime. Germans are fond of meat, particularly pork, and this is normally accompanied by potatoes or other vegetables such as puréed spinach, and salad. The evening meal is simple: a selection of cold sliced meats (*Aufschnitt*) is often served, together with different kinds of bread and cheese. This is washed down with beer or apple juice.

There are many special German dishes, some of which are associated with certain regions or particular times of the year. *Sauerkraut* is popular everywhere. It is a sort of pickled cabbage, and is often served with potatoes, sausages and dumplings which are known as *Knödl*.

Above: Ursula Marschke prepares a meal in her small but well-designed kitchen where everything is easily to hand.

Below: The Marschke family have a breakfast of rolls with jam or cheese. They have milk or coffee to drink.

Special dishes from the south include the famous *Weisswurst* sausages of Munich. Southerners are very fond of asparagus and of trout, and make elaborate cakes. The *Schwarzwälder Kirschtorte* (Black Forest Cherry Cake) has layers of chocolate sponge, spread with black cherry jam and whipped cream.

Along the northern coastline fish and seafood are popular, as is *Labskaus*, or salted meat. *Pumpernickel*, a very dark variety of rye bread, is often served with smoked ham. *Bohnensuppe mit Speck*, a thick bean soup with bacon in it, is just the thing for a winter's day. Lübeck, the port near the East German border, is famous for its marzipan.

Take-away snacks are popular in Germany, especially sausages and french fries (chips) served with mayonnaise or ketchup. The Germans also enjoy eating out, and many towns have Italian, Greek and Turkish restaurants run by some of the immigrant families who have come to Germany.

Below: Dieter Wetzel runs an hotel and restaurant near Stuttgart. As well as cooking, he must find time to welcome his guests.

Pastimes and sports

The mountains and forests of West Germany provide a wealth of opportunity for outdoor activities. Even city dwellers normally have woodlands within easy reach, where they can go for a Sunday walk, or jog along the *Trimm-dich-Pfade* or "keep-fit trails."

Towns of all sizes have open-air and indoor swimming pools: there are a total of about 3,000 in West Germany. In summer everyone who can flocks to the nearest river or lake or drives up to the north coast and islands for a day on the beach. There are sailing and rowing boats everywhere and windsurfing is extremely popular.

The Germans are great gardening enthusiasts and will lovingly tend window-boxes and indoor plants even if they have no garden. Allotments (rented plots of land on which to grow vegetables) are to be found on the outskirts of most towns, and sometimes these include a small summer-house where one may spend evenings and weekends. Sundays are for visiting relatives or the countryside.

Above: Many Germans enjoy skiing on the fine ski slopes to be found in the mountains of Bavaria.

Left: At this popular North Sea resort, most of the families have hired "beach baskets." These provide shelter against the wind.

Left: The Germans are keen soccer fans, and millions of people watch the matches live or on the television. This game is taking place at Düsseldorf.

Below: Germans enjoy both watching and participating in gymnastics. These girls are giving a display of synchronized trampolining at an open-air event.

Soccer is West Germany's most popular sport. Teams such as *Bayern Munich* are well known all over the world, and the German Football Association has more than four million members.

The second most popular sport, and the one with the longest tradition in Germany, is gymnastics. This is followed by shooting, athletics and handball. West Germany made its mark on the world of tennis in 1985, when Boris Becker won the Wimbledon men's singles championship at the age of only 17. Sports like horse-riding, which were once the privilege of the wealthy, are now very popular throughout West Germany.

Every fourth German is a member of a sports club, or *Verein*. Even small villages may have a sports club whose members meet once a week and train in the gymnasium of the local school. Many youngsters join sports clubs as well, because in West Germany there is less emphasis on sport in schools.

News and entertainment

Publishing has long been an important industry in Germany. Printing was invented in Germany in the 15th century, and even today every tenth book published in the world is written in the German language. Books from all over the world are also translated into German: no wonder that reading rates as one of the Germans' most popular pastimes.

Each day around 25 million newspapers are sold in West Germany. The tabloid *Bild Zeitung*, with its sensational headlines, alone attracts almost six million regular readers. There are hardly any national daily papers: most of Germany's famous quality newspapers, such as the *Kölner Stadt-Anzeiger*, are based on one large city.

One can buy a great number of magazines, ranging from political commentaries, such as *Der Spiegel*, to motoring journals, women's and pop music magazines.

Above: Germany has a large number of bright and lively magazines which cater for young readers.

Above: News and women's magazines are the most widely read of the 7,000 periodicals published in West Germany.

Above: News and women's magazines are the most widely read of the 9,400 periodicals published in West Germany.

Above: *Der Grosse Preis* is a television quiz program which helps raise money for children's charities.

Left: Elke Kast is a well-known and very popular television announcer.

Right: A West German television magazine.

Below: Young Germans like listening to many kinds of pop music. British and American groups have always been popular, but German pop stars also have many fans.

West Germany is a land of television watchers. Ninety-six per cent of all households own a television set, and more than half of all Germans switch it on every day. There are three channels: two of them offer a nationwide service, whereas the third varies from region to region. There are nine regional broadcasting corporations.

German television does feature commercials, but they only appear during the afternoon and early evening and they are never used to interrupt a program. News, current affairs and excellent documentaries form a large part of television broadcasting time, but the most popular programs tend to be films, entertainment shows and serials. Many of these are taken from British and American sources and the language is dubbed in German.

Many young people are interested in pop music and spend a lot of money buying the latest records. British and American groups have long dominated the pop scene, but in recent years many German groups have in turn made their mark on the German and international hit parades.

Fact file: home life and leisure

Key facts

Population composition: People under 15 years of age make up 15 per cent of the population; people between 15 and 59 make up 64.6 per cent, and people over 60 make up 20.4 per cent.

Average life expectancy at birth: 75 years (1986), as compared with 70 years in 1960. Women make up 52.2 per cent of West Germany's population and, on average, women live to 78 years, which is 6 years longer than the average for men.

Rate of population increase: Between 1960 and 1970 the population of West Germany increased by 0.9 per cent a year, partly because of immigration from East Germany. In the 1970s and 1980s, the country's population steadily decreased.

Family life: The average age at time of marriage is $25\frac{1}{2}$ for men and 23 for women. Families tend to be small, with most couples having one or two children. German workers are entitled to three weeks' vacation a year by law, but most have four or five weeks.

Homes: About equal numbers live in houses and apartments. Home ownership is low (about 10 per cent) but is steadily increasing.

Work: The aveage working week in industry is about $40\frac{1}{2}$ hours' long. The total workforce in 1985 was 26,610,000, including 10,170,000 women and 2,100,000 foreign (or guest) workers. The number of people unemployed in 1986 had reached 2,050,000, or 8 per cent of the total workforce.

Prices: Prices rose by 3.2 per cent per year between 1960 and 1970 and by 4.9 per cent a year between 1970 and 1982. Between 1980 and 1986, however, the annual rate of inflation was 3 per cent.

Religions: About 49 per cent of the people of West Germany are Protestants and 45 per cent are Roman Catholics. The Roman Catholics are concentrated in the south. Jews make up about 0.1 per cent of the population.

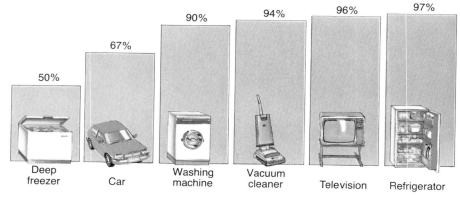

50% Deep freezer
67% Car
90% Washing machine
94% Vacuum cleaner
96% Television
97% Refrigerator

Personal hygiene and health 3%
Other goods and services 3%
Fuel and power 5%
Entertainment and education 8%
Clothing and footwear 10%
Household goods and service 11%
Transport and communications 12%
Housing 16%
Food, alcohol and tobacco 32%

△ **The percentages of households owning various items in the 1980s**
West German families have also acquired many new types of household goods in recent years, such as food processors and microwave ovens.

◁ **How the average household budget is spent**
The West Germans spend more of their income on food than most other Europeans, but the general spending pattern is similar.

▽ **West German currency and stamps**
The basic unit of currency is the Deutsche Mark (DM) which was introduced in 1948. It is divided into 100 Pfennigs. In March 1988 there were about 1.69 DM to the US dollar.

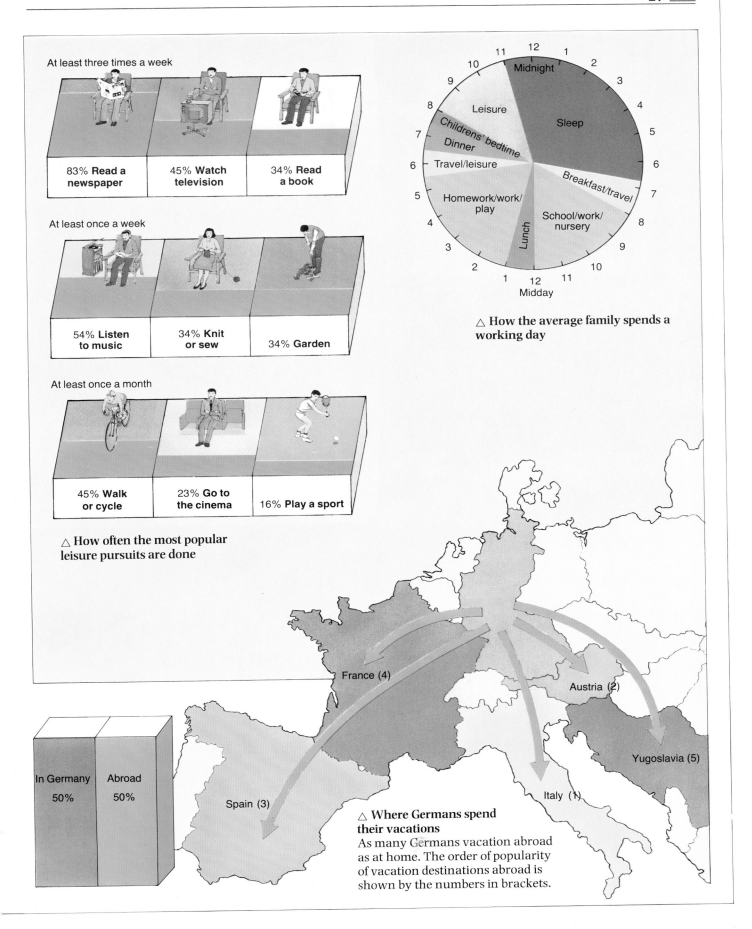

At least three times a week

83% **Read a newspaper**

45% **Watch television**

34% **Read a book**

At least once a week

54% **Listen to music**

34% **Knit or sew**

34% **Garden**

At least once a month

45% **Walk or cycle**

23% **Go to the cinema**

16% **Play a sport**

△ How often the most popular leisure pursuits are done

11 12 1
10 2
9 3
8 Midnight 4
Leisure Sleep
Childrens' bedtime
Dinner
Travel/leisure Breakfast/travel
Homework/work/ School/work/
play nursery
Lunch
Midday

△ How the average family spends a working day

France (4)

Austria (2)

Yugoslavia (5)

Italy (1)

Spain (3)

In Germany 50% | Abroad 50%

△ **Where Germans spend their vacations**
As many Germans vacation abroad as at home. The order of popularity of vacation destinations abroad is shown by the numbers in brackets.

Farming and forestry

The West Germans make full use of almost all the farmland they have available, but the country has fewer fertile areas than some other European countries.

The largest grassland areas are along the North Sea coast and in the foothills of the Alps. These are used for grazing cattle. The coastal region is best known for beef and milk production, the south for its cheeses, butter, and other dairy products.

Northwestern Germany is a mixture of forest, heath, arable and grassland: it produces cereals and potatoes. The Central Uplands are given over to mixed farming. The crops vary according to soil and position, and include wheat, rye, oats, potatoes and sugar beet. The areas around Cologne and the foothills of the Harz Mountains are particularly fertile.

Along the Rhine, and the valleys of the Neckar, Nahe and Mosel (Moselle) rivers, the climate is generally mild, and the soil is suitable for fruit and vines. The vineyards rise in terraces along the sunny sides of the valleys.

Below left: Cheeses are an important product of the German dairy industry.

Below: Typical German livestock breeds.

Above: The Lanx family run a small farm in southern Germany. It is a mixed farm and they have both cereal crops and livestock.

Left: This Bavarian farmer is harvesting maize which will be used for animal foodstuffs. A hop field can be seen in the background. The hops will be used for producing beer.

Below: These vineyards around the Kaiserstuhl, an old volcanic mountain in the Rhine valley, yield particularly good wine grapes.

Most West German farms are not large, so many farmers buy machinery through cooperatives they have set up with other farmers. Most farms are highly mechanized and scientific. Traditional small-holdings continue to exist in many places too, but the income from these often has to be supplemented by wages from another job.

Although fewer and fewer people are being employed in agriculture, and the number of farms is declining, efficiency is improving. West Germany produces about three-quarters of the food it needs, and is almost self-sufficient in wheat, oats, potatoes and dairy products.

In ancient times Germany was covered in dense forests of oak and other broadleaved trees. Today it is famous for its conifers. About 30 million cubic meters (39 million cubic yards) of timber are felled each year, yet large quantities still need to be imported to meet the country's needs. The forests of Germany have been badly affected by industrial pollution.

Natural resources and industry

West Germany has to import large quantities of raw materials, as its own resources are limited. There are some deposits of iron ore, petroleum and natural gas, but the only really substantial reserves are of hard coal and lignite or brown coal. As in all other industrialized countries, the use of energy is always on the increase even though the government tries to encourage people to save fuel.

The largest coalfields are in the Ruhr area, which in the last century became Europe's most important industrial region. When cheaper fuels became available, many of the coal mines were closed down. All the remaining ones have been merged into one enormous company. There are also substantial coal deposits in the Saar region, near Germany's border with France.

Today, coal only accounts for a third of the country's energy consumption, whereas petroleum accounts for nearly a half. West Germany's few oilfields can cater for only a fraction of its needs. However, about 40 per cent of natural gas used does come from German fields.

Above: Lignite, a type of coal, is excavated at this open-cast mine in Garsdorf in the Ruhr district of western Germany.

Below: This nuclear power station in north Bavaria helps to meet Germany's increasing energy demands.

Above: Well-known German car manufacturers' symbols.

Left: A view inside the BMW factory in Munich.

Below: Part of a huge steelworks in Saarland, in western Germany.

Coal, water and nuclear energy are all used to produce electricity. West Germany has many hydroelectric power stations but the largest ones are in the south. Some are jointly operated with Austria and Switzerland.

West Germany produces more iron and steel than any other European country. The main plants are situated near the coalfields of the Ruhr and Saar regions. The production of heavy machinery has always played an important part in the German economy. Machine manufacture today accounts for 10 per cent of the country's industrial turnover, and employs more than a million people.

After the USA and Japan, West Germany is the third largest car producer in the world. It was in Germany that the two inventors, Gottlieb Daimler and Karl Benz, built the first car in 1885. Today such names as Volkswagen, Audi, BMW and Mercedes are household names throughout the world.

Manufacturing industries

West Germany's imports of many of the raw materials needed by its industries are balanced by exports of manufactured goods and, in fact, approximately a quarter of the German workforce produces goods which will be exported. Goods from Germany are available all over the world and are generally regarded as being advanced in their technology, reliable, of good quality and well finished.

Cars are the best-known German product and the motor industry used to be the largest. Today, however, the chemical industry takes first place in the manufacturing sector. It employs a workforce of nearly 600,000, and of these, 80 per cent work for the three leading companies, BASF, Hoechst and Bayer. They produce an enormous range of products, from paints and plastics to cosmetics and medicines.

The electrical engineering industry, too, is very important. Siemens, Braun, Miele, AEG and Bosch are just some of the well-known names. Among many other items, they produce kitchen equipment, televisions and hi-fi sets.

Above: This woman is packing hairdriers and their accessories on a Braun factory production line.

Below: This refinery which is situated near Mannheim is part of BASF, the largest chemical company in the country.

Keeping up with modern developments, German companies also produce a wide range of office and data-processing equipment such as typewriters and computers.

Textiles are Germany's oldest-established industry and, despite considerable decline, clothes manufacturing is still the most important of all the consumer goods industries. Other traditional German products include precision instruments, china and glass.

The majority of the workforce is employed in very large enterprises which also account for more than half of the total industrial output. Yet many companies are very small, employing fewer than 50 people. Manufacturing output and productivity increased steadily during the 1960s and 1970s, because of the investment of large sums of money. In recent years, as a result of the world economic recession, the number of enterprises has been falling steadily, yet Germany continues to be Europe's leading industrial power.

Above: At the annual Hanover Trade Fair about 5,500 exhibitors display the newest industrial products.

Below: This small factory makes high quality knitwear for sale throughout West Germany.

Transportation

West Germany is a land dominated by the motor car. Four-fifths of all passenger transportation is by car, and it is the most common means of getting to work or going on vacation.

Germany was one of the first countries in the world to build a motorway (*Autobahn*) network, and today only the USA has more motorways. Although West Germany already has the densest motorway network in the world, it is planning to extend it even further, so that by 1990 85 per cent of the population should live within 10 km (6 miles) of a motorway.

On public holidays and in the summer the *Autobahnen* are very congested, partly because of local traffic, and partly because they are used by motorists from other north European countries who want to travel south.

The Federal German Railroad (*Deutsche Bundesbahn*) has some 27,500 km (17,100 miles) of track, about 11,000 km (6,835 miles) of which is electrified; the latter carries about 84 per cent of all rail traffic.

Above: Some 80 per cent of West Germany's goods are carried by road. There is an extensive network of *Autobahnen* and other roads in Germany.

Below: German railroads are being modernized, and people are being encouraged to travel by train rather than use private cars.

Cross-country buses are usually run by the railroad company or by the post office (*Deutsche Bundespost*). Within towns there are municipal bus services and trams (*Strassenbahnen*). An increasing number of cities have an underground (*U-Bahn*) network, which is often an extension of the existing tram system. There are no conductors on trams and buses and one has to buy tickets from a machine before starting a journey.

The national airline of West Germany is Lufthansa. In 1986 it carried about 43 million passengers and 800,000 tons of freight. Lufthansa is based at Frankfurt am Main, which has one of the largest and busiest airports in Europe.

West Germany has more than 4,000 km (2,500 miles) of inland waterways which are used for freight traffic. Canals, and rivers such as the Rhine, are busy with tugs and strings of barges, as well as with flag-bedecked pleasure craft.

Above: Frankfurt is one of 11 large civil airports located throughout West Germany. Over 75 airlines fly in and out of German airports.

Below: A barge on the Rhine. Inland waterways account for about a quarter of long-distance goods transport in West Germany.

Fact file: economy and trade

Key facts

Structure of production: Of the total GDP (the value of all economic activity in West Germany), farming, forestry and fishing contribute 2 per cent, industry 40 per cent, and services 58 per cent.

Farming: Farmland covers roughly half of West Germahy. *Main products:* Barley, wheat, fruit, wine grapes, hops, oats, potatoes, rye, sugar beet. *Livestock:* Cattle, 15,806,000; pigs, 23,905,000; sheep, 1,779,000; poultry, 72,124,000.

Forestry and fishing: Forests cover about a quarter of West Germany. In 1986, the fishing fleet contained 648 cutters, 15 trawlers and 1 lugger.

Mining: West Germany is the world's ninth largest coal producer and it ranks third in lignite (brown coal) production. Potash, some iron ore and oil are also mined, but West Germany imports many minerals and oil.

Energy: Of the total electrical energy produced in 1984, power stations using coal, gas or oil contributed 79 per cent, nuclear power stations 13 per cent, and hydroelectric stations 8 per cent.

Manufacturing: West Germany ranks fourth in the world in industrial production, after the USA, the USSR and Japan.

Transportation; *Roads:* 173,240 km (107,649 miles), including 8,350 km (5,189 miles) of *Autobahn*; *Rail:* 27,484 km (17,078 miles); *Waterways:* 4,429 km (2,752 miles); *Shipping:* The merchant fleet included 1,950 ocean-going vessels in 1986; *Air:* The national airline is Lufthansa.

Trade (1987): *Total imports:* US $217,065 million; *exports:* US $286,413 million. This makes West Germany the world's second most important trading nation.

Economic growth: The average growth rate of West Germany's gross national product between the years of 1980 and 1987 was 1.9 per cent a year.

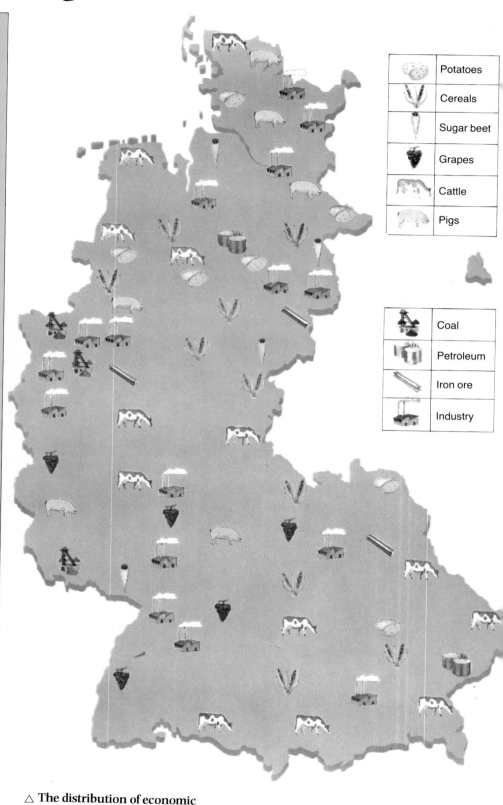

	Potatoes
	Cereals
	Sugar beet
	Grapes
	Cattle
	Pigs

	Coal
	Petroleum
	Iron ore
	Industry

△ **The distribution of economic activity in West Germany**

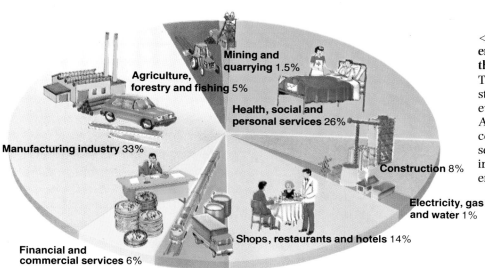

Mining and quarrying 1.5%

Agriculture, forestry and fishing 5%

Health, social and personal services 26%

Manufacturing industry 33%

Construction 8%

Electricity, gas and water 1%

Shops, restaurants and hotels 14%

Financial and commercial services 6%

Transport and communications 5.5%

◁ **The percentages of the workforce employed in various industries in the 1980s**
The largest industrial employer is still the manufacturing industry even with the economic recession. As in many other Western countries, employment in the service industries is tending to increase while the numbers employed in agriculture decrease.

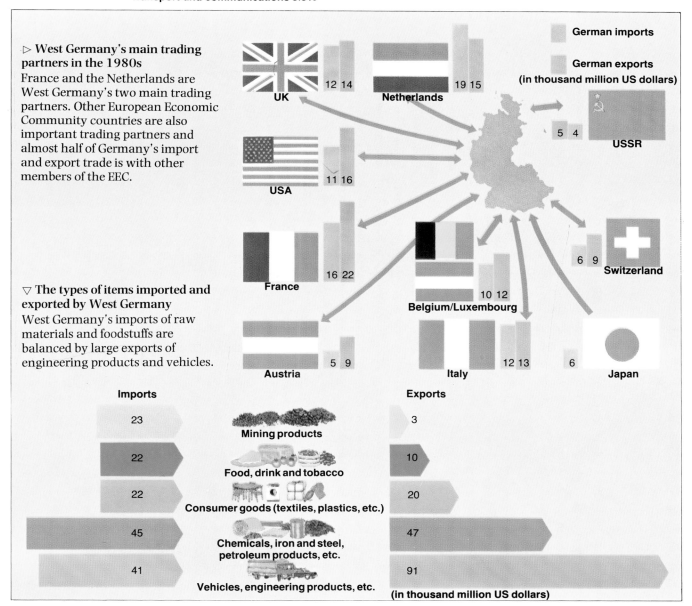

▷ **West Germany's main trading partners in the 1980s**
France and the Netherlands are West Germany's two main trading partners. Other European Economic Community countries are also important trading partners and almost half of Germany's import and export trade is with other members of the EEC.

German imports

German exports
(in thousand million US dollars)

UK 12 14

Netherlands 19 15

USA 11 16

USSR 5 4

France 16 22

Switzerland 6 9

Belgium/Luxembourg 10 12

▽ **The types of items imported and exported by West Germany**
West Germany's imports of raw materials and foodstuffs are balanced by large exports of engineering products and vehicles.

Austria 5 9

Italy 12 13

Japan 6

Imports		Exports
23	Mining products	3
22	Food, drink and tobacco	10
22	Consumer goods (textiles, plastics, etc.)	20
45	Chemicals, iron and steel, petroleum products, etc.	47
41	Vehicles, engineering products, etc.	91

(in thousand million US dollars)

Education

Education in West Germany is organized individually by each Federal State. The type of school attended by a child, and what he or she learns there, depends on where the school is situated.

Even so, the broad pattern remains the same throughout the country. Education is free for everyone from primary school through to university. All children have to attend school for 12 years, of which nine need to be full time, and of which the last three can be part time. Schools are often run on informal lines; there are no school uniforms and children are encouraged to be independent.

The first four years of school are spent at primary school (*Grundschule*). There are then several options. In order to postpone a decision, many pupils now spend their fifth and sixth years in a so-called "orientation grade." Some then opt for intermediate schooling in a *Realschule* which takes six years and leads to an exam for entrance into technical college.

Above: When the weather is fine pupils spend their breaks in the yard in front of their large modern school situated north of Munich.

Below: These children at a school in Cologne are taking part in an English lesson. All Germans must study a foreign language at school.

Left: These apprentices at vocational school are studying the properties of some of the materials used in the printing industry.

Below: Bonn University was founded in 1786. There are about a million students at German universities, which is more than five times the number in the early 1960s.

About half of all pupils go on to a short-course secondary school (*Hauptschule*) until they are 15 years old, when they take up a vocational apprenticeship (*Lehre*). These last three years and there are about 450 professions to choose from. Most of the training is on the job, but there are also lessons on general subjects, such as German, English and mathematics, as well as on the theoretical side of the work.

Would-be teachers or university students must go to a grammar school, or *Gymnasium*. Some of these specialize in the arts, others in sciences, but they all require nine years' attendance before taking the final *Abitur* exam. The top class, or *Oberprima*, will, therefore, often have pupils who are 20 years old or more.

The trouble with this system is that it is very hard for a pupil to change from one type of school to another in midstream. Therefore a number of Federal States have introduced comprehensive schools (*Gesamtschulen*) for all pupils from the fifth school year onwards.

The arts

Probably no other country has produced as many outstanding composers as Germany. Johann Sebastian Bach (1685–1750), Ludwig van Beethoven (1770–1827) and Richard Wagner (1813–83) are just a few of the many famous names to be associated with classical music. Today, music remains a popular part of German cultural life. Even small towns have concert halls, and often a municipal orchestra as well. Major orchestras, such as the Berlin Philharmonic, are internationally famous.

Those who prefer dramatic arts also have no lack of choice. Almost all the theaters in West Germany are publicly owned and are subsidized so that they do not have to support themselves solely by the sale of tickets. Each year around 17 million people go to see a play in Germany. The classical German playwrights are Johann Wolfgang von Goethe, whose greatest dramatic achievement was *Faust*, Johann von Schiller (1759–1805) and Gotthold Ephraim Lessing (1729–81), and their works are the ones most frequently performed.

Above: Ludwig van Beethoven ranks as one of the greatest classical composers. He wrote symphonies, concertos and chamber music.

Left: A scene from the opera *Tannhäuser*. This was written by Richard Wagner, the master of German romantic opera.

German writers are probably less well known than German composers, though the literature is very rich, and every century has produced some outstanding works. Bertolt Brecht (1898–1956) and Thomas Mann (1875–1955) are the best known this century, and their books have been translated into many other languages. During the Hitler regime the arts were suppressed generally, so the end of World War II marked a new beginning, with writers such as Günter Grass (1927–) and Heinrich Böll (1917–) becoming very popular.

Although there is no great tradition of German painting, a few artists, such as the Renaissance painter Albrecht Dürer (1471–1528) produced outstanding works. There was also an important painting revival, the expressionist movement, at the beginning of the 20th century.

In recent years films from Germany have begun to reach international acclaim. *The Tin Drum* and *The Marriage of Maria Braun*, for instance, have been shown in many countries throughout the world.

Above left: The poet and playwright Goethe (1749–1832).

Above: Albrecht Dürer's painting *The Virgin and Child*.

Below: Despite war-time losses, some of Germany's fine architecture survived. The famous Gothic cathedral in Cologne was started in 1248, but was not completed until 1880.

The making of modern Germany

Until the middle of the 19th century, Germany consisted of numerous separate states. During the middle years of the century, the state of Prussia, under Wilhelm I and his prime minister Otto von Bismarck, became the leader in the move towards unification. After a series of wars in which Prussia and its allies annexed parts of Denmark, Austria and France, Germany was finally united in 1871. Wilhelm I became Emperor of the new German Empire. Under Wilhelm II (1888–1918), Germany was led into a disasterous war in 1914.

World War I (1914–18) ended in defeat for Germany and her allies. The Empire ended, and Germany became a republic. In 1919 a new constitution was drawn up but the republic never reached a firm footing. It collapsed in 1929, during the world economic crisis. No majority capable of governing could be found, and the previously almost unknown National Socialist movement under Adolf Hitler grew to be the strongest party within two years.

Above: Bismarck was known as the "Iron Chancellor." He held much power in Germany in the second half of the 19th century, but was not a democratic leader.

Left: The prospect of a unified Germany was a threat to France, and one of the reasons for the Franco-German war in 1870. Here the Prussian artillery are laying siege to the city of Strasbourg.

Left: A German soldier at an observation post in World War I. Nearly two million German soldiers were killed in this war.

Above: Adolf Hitler (1889–1945).

Below: World War II left Berlin in ruins.

In January 1933 Hitler became Reich Chancellor and he proceeded to give himself almost unlimited power. Opposition parties were banned and citizens' freedoms were strongly curtailed. Political opponents and Jews in particular were persecuted. Those who did not manage to escape were taken to concentration camps where millions of them were killed. In spite of all this there was very little opposition to Hitler's dictatorship because he had promised the Germans an improved economy and no more unemployment.

It was Hitler's aim to conquer all of Europe, and his attack on Poland in September 1939 marked the beginning of World War II. Although the German army was successful early in the war, it soon began to suffer serious losses. However, the war continued until April 1945 when the entire country was occupied by enemies. Hitler killed himself and Germany surrendered to the Allied Powers who divided it into four military occupation zones. It was an enormous defeat and left the country in ruins.

West Germany in the modern world

West Germany as we know it today is a very young country. It came into existence in May 1949, when a new "Basic Law" was drawn up. Elections for parliament (*Bundestag*) were held for the first time in August 1949 and Konrad Adenauer became the first Federal Chancellor. Even then, however, the ultimate power lay with the occupying forces and Germany only became a sovereign country in 1955. From the outset it was the aim of the West German government to re-create a united Germany. Yet the country has remained divided and although relations between East and West have improved, there has been no real solution to this problem.

After the large-scale destruction during World War II, Germans immediately began to rebuild their country. In the 1950s and 1960s, Germany experienced an economic boom.

The economic boom also brought with it many problems. When there was a shortage of workers, many foreigners were encouraged to come and work in West German industry. However, no real attempt was made to make them feel at home.

Below left: In recent years Turks and other immigrant workers have protested about their poor living conditions.

Above: Adenauer (right) meets De Gaulle in 1963.
Below: Chancellor Kohl (right) at a meeting with the Italian Prime Minister in 1983.

Left: Members of the German environmental or "Green" party in front of a dummy rocket used to protest in 1982 about German nuclear policy.

Above: Pollution is a problem in many German rivers.
Below: This German street shows many foreign influences.

More recently there has been a recession in Germany, as in most Western countries, and many people are unemployed.

Many Germans – especially young people – are very critical of the society in which they live. They want more from life than money and well-being. Large numbers of people are taking a great interest in environmental issues and this is reflected in the growing support for ecologically orientated parties such as the "Greens".

Many foreign influences – especially American ones – affect everyday life in Germany. People wear jeans, yet it is not unusual, especially on special occasions, to see someone in traditional dress. People listen to English or American pop music, but they also celebrate the age-old festivals. The Germans are happy with this mixture of traditional and modern ways and few would consider leaving the country to live elsewhere.

Fact file: government and world role

Key facts

Official name: *Bundesrepublik Deutschland* (Federal Republic of Germany).

Flag: Three horizontal bars of black, red and gold.

National anthem: The third verse of *Deutschland-Lied*.

National government: *Head of State:* The President, who is elected by the Federal Convention for a term of 5 years. *Head of the government:* The Federal Chancellor, who is proposed by the President and elected by the *Bundestag. Parliament:* The 498 voting members of the *Bundestag* are directly elected. There are also 22 non-voting members from West Berlin. The Federal Council (*Bundesrat*) consists of members of the ten states, or *Länder*. Most legislation passed by the *Bundestag* must then go to be approved by the *Bundesrat* before it finally becomes law.

Local government: Each of the ten *Länder* has regional government. Nine have a one-house legislature, but Bavaria has two houses. The city of West Berlin has the privileges of a state and it elects a house of representatives. However, the final authority in West Berlin rests in the Western Allies.

Armed forces: *Army:* The strength of the Army in 1988 was 332,100, including 175,900 draftees. There is compulsory military service for 18 months. *Air Force:* The Air Force consisted of 108,700 people in 1988. *Navy:* The Navy had 38,500 personnel in 1988.

Economic alliances: West Germany was one of the founder members of the European Economic Community (or Common Market) in 1957. The aims of the EEC are to bring a closer union between the peoples of Europe and to provide economic expansion. The EEC is now the world's largest trading bloc.

Political alliances: West Germany is a member of the UN, the Council of Europe and, since 1953, the North Atlantic Treaty Organization (NATO).

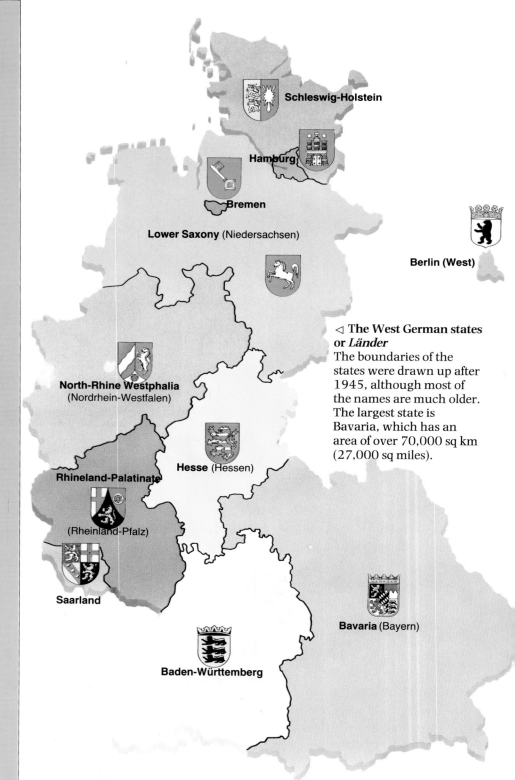

Schleswig-Holstein

Hamburg

Bremen

Lower Saxony (Niedersachsen)

North-Rhine Westphalia (Nordrhein-Westfalen)

Rhineland-Palatinate (Rheinland-Pfalz)

Saarland

Hesse (Hessen)

Baden-Württemberg

Bavaria (Bayern)

Berlin (West)

◁ **The West German states or *Länder***
The boundaries of the states were drawn up after 1945, although most of the names are much older. The largest state is Bavaria, which has an area of over 70,000 sq km (27,000 sq miles).

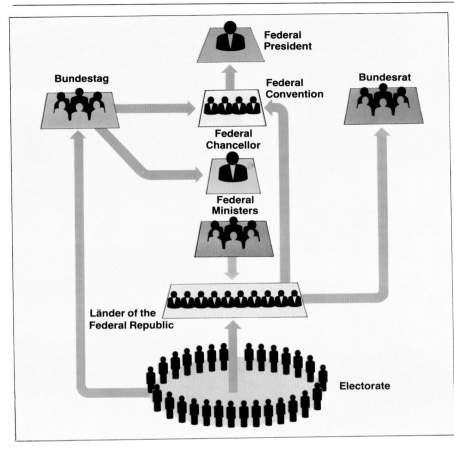

Federal President

Bundestag

Federal Convention

Bundesrat

Federal Chancellor

Federal Ministers

Länder of the Federal Republic

Electorate

◁ **The government of West Germany**
The federal system of government of West Germany is similar to that of the United States. The *Länder* (or States) have wide powers but some major functions, such as defense, are executed only by the federal government. The Federal Chancellor is the leader of the largest political party in the *Bundestag* (Parliament).

Australia 10,900

Belgium 11,360

Canada 15,080

France 12,860

West Germany 14,460

Italy 10,420

Japan 15,770

Netherlands 11,860

New Zealand 8,230

Spain 6,010

UK 10,430

USA 18,430

(in US dollars)

△ **National wealth created per person in 1987**
West Germany's national wealth increased rapidly during the 1960s and 1970s. Although the growth rate has slowed recently, West Germany is still Europe's wealthiest nation.

▽ **The European Economic Community**
The EEC has now grown from six to twelve members. Many trade barriers have been abolished between members, and there are common policies for agriculture and fisheries.

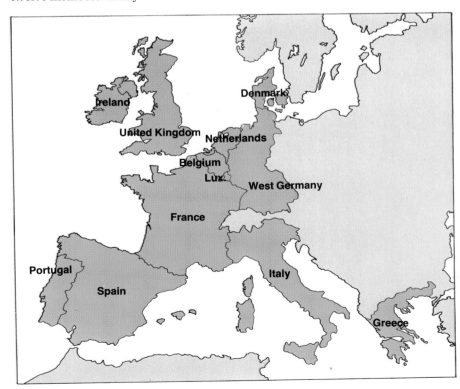

Ireland, Denmark, United Kingdom, Netherlands, Belgium, Lux., West Germany, France, Portugal, Spain, Italy, Greece

Index